How to Make Money on the Internet

Leave Your 9 to 5 Job and Create a Passive Income in 2020

Author

Table Of Contents

Introduction

The world we live in today is different from the world we lived in 30 years ago for many reasons. Some of the differences are negative in that we are struggling with challenges such as climate change and overpopulation, but so many of the differences are positive. The advent of the internet has changed the world. Suddenly, information that was only accessible to a rare few became accessible to the entire world. Communication became instantaneous, and for businesses, their market was suddenly not only local but international. This also opened up a whole new arena for entrepreneurs to work within. E-commerce was born and with it the E-preneur. E-Commerce is defined as any commercial transaction that takes place electronically on the internet. This includes any website or application where a purchase of any product can be made. An E-preneur is an entrepreneur who uses the power of the internet and E-commerce to run businesses and generate revenue. E-Commerce is a $ 1.2 trillion business worldwide, and this number is set to increase by a minimum of 15 percent per year (Lucrazon, n.d.).

In *How to Make Money on the Internet,* we will teach you the skills to get your slice of the revenue pie. Also, we seek to teach you skills to build online businesses that will eventually run themselves. If that sounds too good to be true, then you have likely never encountered the concept of passive income.

Passive income is income that is generated with little to no daily effort from the recipient. Examples include things like rental properties, but for the purposes of this book, we will focus on passive income through E-commerce methods. The idea is to build as many passive income streams as possible so that the bulk of your income comes from avenues that you are not required to work on daily. Through the building of a passive income portfolio, you can achieve financial freedom. Let us be clear that this does not mean you will be retiring at 30 and never have to work a day in your life again. Passive income streams take time and work to create and build, and they do still require occasional interaction to maintain. What you are doing is creating a safety net. When the economy takes a slide or life throws a curveball at you, you will be far more likely to bounce back with little permanent financial impact on you and your family.

The key is to start as soon as you can. Don't leave building passive income until "you have time," as I can guarantee that you will never have a portion of time magically appear. If building a passive income portfolio is important enough to you, you will need to take the time to put in the work, right now. After all, the sooner you start, the sooner you will start seeing the financial rewards.

Financial freedom may sound like a dream that only the very lucky get to experience. This is not true. Financial freedom means that you can maintain your lifestyle without a regular paycheck. In other words, you are not financially bound to one company or employer to provide you with the monthly financial means to survive and thrive.

Along with financial freedom comes the freedom of location and time. When you are not bound to one specific form of active income, i.e., a permanent job, you have the freedom to use your time as you please, and as the source of your income is internet-based, you are able to work from anywhere as long as you have an internet connection.

In *How to Make Money on the Internet,* we will introduce you to the various methods that you can use to create your passive income portfolio, and we will also delve into how you can arrive at those methods. A very specific mindset is required to achieve success in passive income generation, and we will discuss what this mindset entails. We will provide you with five different passive income business ideas to use in 2020 and go in-depth into the method we recommend most highly—affiliate marketing.

If the idea of being financially free and being able to choose where and when you work sounds good to you, then read on, as your future awaits you.

Chapter 1: The E-Preneur Mindset

A large part of success in E-commerce and the building of a passive income portfolio is your mindset. Thankfully, that is something that you can control.

As with any business, building an E-business take self-discipline and commitment. You need to completely commit yourself to the journey so that when you reach the inevitable, occasional obstacle, you are mentally strong enough to overcome them.

Building any business never happens overnight, and the same is true for online businesses. A great image to use to imagine what building a business is like is the Success Iceberg. When you look at an iceberg, no matter how big it may be, the part that you see above the water is actually a very small portion of the iceberg as a whole. The biggest portion of the iceberg is underwater, and you can't see it. Business is the same. The portion of a business that you see in the world, no matter how large, is only the end-product. The part that you don't see is all the hard work, tears, frustration, and persistence that it took to create that business. As you enter your online business journey, this is something that you need to understand and accept. If hard work scares you, then you are likely better off continuing to work for a boss. This is not to say that you cannot work smart and in this way reduce the hard work.

Planning is also a very important part of your mindset. It may be tempting to just jump into an idea without researching it thoroughly as the excitement takes hold of you. Unfortunately, businesses that are not properly researched and planned are doomed to fail. Luckily, we've done a lot of the research for you in *How to Make Money on the Internet* and other titles in our range, so by purchasing this book, you've already made a huge leap in the right direction.

Once you have committed yourself to the hard work involved and properly researched and planned your idea, the next most important part of your online business building journey is visualizing your dream. Words are important, but pictures and feelings impact the mind far more significantly. As part of your mental preparation for your journey, you will want to visualize what it is going to be like to have your passive income portfolio up and running. You have to close your eyes to do this to avoid any distractions and then picture in your mind what your idea of success will be like. Don't just picture generalities, picture details. What will you feel like—other than just happy? What will you be doing? How will you be doing it? How will your loved ones be impacted? What value will you be adding to the world? This visualization is going to be your constant sounding board. Any time you feel like giving up, remember what that success felt and looked like. If you are generally not very good at self-motivating, this step is going to be key for you because if you do it well, it will, without fail, re-motivate you at every step.

Positivity is not a nice-to-have when you are building an E-business; it is a necessity. If you allow negativity to start dragging you down, you will give up, and sadly, you will never know how close you were to success because quitting is permanent. Imagine a treasure hunter digging a tunnel that he believes leads to a chest of gold. The digging is tiring, and the ground is hard. The treasure hunter becomes exhausted, and eventually, after days of digging, he convinces himself that he's wasting his time and walks away from the tunnel he's already dug. Later that same day, another treasure hunter comes along and continues digging that same tunnel. After removing just two shovels of dirt, he hits the treasure chest and he's a millionaire. When the first treasure hunter gave up, he had no idea how close he was to success. Every time you feel like giving up, think about the fact that you could be just two shovels of dirt away from your goal.

You will never be able to plan for every eventuality, but it is important to have a general idea of where you are going and how you are going to get there. You can do this by developing a business roadmap. Just like roadmaps that we use to get us from one point to another, a business roadmap is intended to get you from your existing point to your ideal end-point. You can plot out very general stages for your business roadmap that could include:

- Acquiring resources
- Building your website
- Monetizing your website

- Acquiring your revenue
- Delivering value to your customers

By building this roadmap, you give yourself an overview of what to expect so that you can mentally prepare yourself for each stage, and you can know in advance if you may need to call in help for anything.

Asking for help is something all successful entrepreneurs do. Successful entrepreneurs understand their strengths and their weaknesses, and they are willing to allow others to handle the parts of their business-building processes that they know are better outsourced. A successful entrepreneur does not pretend to be an expert in all things, and although you need to be willing to ask for help, that does not mean that you lose ownership of the success of what others are doing for you. Ask for help, but always remember that the ultimate responsibility lies with you.

It can be easy to get lost in the planning and preparation stages and simply never get going. An action mindset is vitally important to an entrepreneur.

Do not allow yourself to be fooled; there is a major shift in mindset required in the transition from being an employee to being an entrepreneur, and some are not capable of making that shift. Understanding your own motivation is important. Why do you want to do this? If your answer is "to make money," that's not good enough. Why do you want to make money? What do you want to do with it? Is it really money you want or something that money can buy you, like freedom or more time with your family? Once you fully and deeply understand your motivation, you can continually refer to that so you can keep yourself going in difficult times.

Be prepared to make slow progress and celebrate the small wins. You will soon become unmotivated if you plan only to be happy when you're making money from your business. Celebrate every accomplishment along the way as every step is moving you toward your goal.

Allow yourself to make mistakes. You will never learn anything if you don't do anything incorrectly the first time. Mistakes are merely stepping stones to success. In the same vein, it is vital to remain teachable and learn continuously. Get yourself into the habit of learning and applying that knowledge and then learn something else and apply that too. In this way, you won't consume reams of material and forget everything the minute you start your business.

Keep in mind that the whole point of what you are doing is so you can enjoy your life. By the same token, you should enjoy your business. Do your best to choose an area of E-commerce that you are passionate about and excites you. If you do what you love, you will never work a day in your life.

To maintain this mindset, you need to ensure that you surround yourself with like-minded people. Join E-commerce groups on social media or attend networking breakfasts. Speak to other people who are on the same journey. Not only will you no longer feel so alone, but you will undoubtedly get fresh ideas and find solutions to some of your problems. Having a mentor, if possible, is great as well. Try to find someone you can look up to, and even if you are only following them on social media or YouTube and not having personal contact with them, you will always have something to aspire to. It also helps to know that even the most successful people started somewhere.

Don't allow yourself to get so caught up in the process that you don't pause for a minute to look back at how far you've come. Be proud of yourself, accept congratulations from others, and enjoy your success. Then allow that moment to fire you up to continue going further and achieving more (Anderson, 2018).

Chapter 2: The Top 5 Passive Income Businesses to Start in 2020

Now that you have put yourself into the right mindset to be a successful E-preneur, you can consider the options that you have to make passive income. Options for passive income are developing daily. In this chapter, we will present five of the most popular and well-established methods of earning passive income. We will explain the pros and cons of each method and give you an indication of how long it could take for you to start earning money from each method.

Amazon FBA

What Is It?

The letters "FBA" in the name of this method stand for Fulfilment by Amazon. The idea behind this method is that you have a product to sell and Amazon stocks and sells it for you and then pays you the proceeds to you.

How Does It Work?

If you have a physical product you wish to sell, you will send the items to Amazon. They will stock it in one of their warehouses, and when a customer orders one of the items, Amazon will pick, pack, and ship it on your behalf. They will also handle any returns and refunds.

What Resources Do You Need?

You only need the physical product that you want to sell. These can be new items that your business makes, or it can be second-hand items. It depends on the business you are in. You will need to be able to log in to Amazon's website regularly to ensure that your inventory is kept up-to-date. Depending on how highly your products rank on the website, you may or may not need to do additional advertising and marketing. You must also be aware that you are responsible for sales tax. When your product is being purchased out of different warehouses across different states, it can be challenging to calculate exactly how much sales tax you should be paying.

Advantages

The advantage of using Amazon FBA to sell your products is that you are placing your them on an E-commerce marketplace that has a substantial customer base. Also, you don't need to invest in an E-commerce store or website as you will be using Amazon's site. You save time and money because you won't need to handle the processing and shipping of orders. Amazon is one of the most advanced E-commerce fulfillment services in the world, and it is known for excellent customer service.

Disadvantages

One of the disadvantages, of course, is that this service is not free. Amazon charges you storage and fulfillment fees, so even if you are not selling, you still have the storage expense. Also,you don't get paid for your sale immediately. Amazon pays its sellers every two weeks. With Amazon handling your returns (and their returns process being so easy), you may see more returns of your product. Amazon has strict guidelines on how to prepare your product before it is shipped to the buyer, and it can take some getting used to (Carragher, n.d.).

How Long Before I Make Money?

This is a difficult question to answer as it really depends on how long it takes for you to get your first sale. If you get your first sale the minute your products go live Amazon's website, then you'll earn money within two weeks, but it can take a few weeks or even months for your products to gain traction.

Kindle Direct Publishing

What Is It?

Kindle Direct Publishing (KDP) is a self-publishing service for digital books through Amazon. It allows you to self-publish your book without any outside assistance and sell it on the Amazon website.

How Does It Work?

The logical first step is to have a book written in e-Book format and formatted to Amazon's requirements. The next step is to create a Kindle Direct Publishing account. You will then follow all of the information required by the KDP system, which includes your book's title, information about the book, and a book description. You will be required to select seven keywords that buyers can use to search for books that fit a topic or genre. You will be required to select two categories into which your book falls. You are then required to upload your book cover and the file containing your manuscript. The final step is to set your pricing, then click 'publish,' and you are done.

What Resources Do You Need?

A book written and formatted to KDP specifications (which can be found on their website) is the primary resource. It is imperative to ensure that you are putting out a quality product, so even if you are a proficient writer, it is important to have a qualified editor edit your book before publishing. You will also need a well-designed digital book cover (also formatted to KDP specifications). You will need to do a significant amount of advertising and marketing of your own in the beginning so that the world can be made aware of your fantastic new book. Once you have an existing following, this becomes easier, but your first book will undoubtedly take a significant amount of marketing to get the sales rolling.

Advantages

The main advantage of using KDP is that you can publish your book without going through a publishing house or other type of self-publishing business. The KDP process is free, and you will receive a higher percentage of your book-sale profit than you would if you published traditionally. Of course, having your book on the Amazon website is a huge benefit in and of itself as they have an amazing reach.

Disadvantages

The reading public is well-aware that books sold through KDP have not been through a traditional publishing process, which includes vetting of the manuscript and editing, so they rely heavily on the reviews to judge the quality of a book before they buy it. It is up to you to encourage as many people as possible to review your book and give it a high rating. This form of publishing requires a huge amount of initial work from the author in terms of advertising and marketing. To generate sales and reviews, you will most likely need to offer the book at a very low price for an initial period.

How Long Before I Make Money?

KDP pays authors 60 days after the month the royalties are earned. If you sell a book in August, you will be paid your portion for that sale in October. There is, however, a minimum threshold that you need to earn before KDP will pay you (Awosika, 2019).

Affiliate Marketing

What Is It?

Generally speaking, affiliate marketing is an agreement made between an online retailer and an external website owner to pay commission for traffic or sales directed to the online retailer from the external website. Many different online retailers offer affiliate agreements, including Amazon. Affiliate marketing is the easiest and most popular method of earning passive income. Essentially, you are promoting another company's product and earning a commission if a customer purchases through a referral from you.

How Does It Work?

Once your website, blog, YouTube channel or podcast is set up, you will apply to online retailers to be included in their affiliate program. How you advertise your affiliate's products and how your sales will be tracked depends on the nature of your platform. If you have a website or blog, your affiliate partner will most likely provide you with specialized links to embed on your site when you advertise their product. When a visitor to your website or blog clicks on that link, it will take them to the affiliate's website. If they purchase the item, your referral links will be tracked with that transaction, and your affiliate partner will be notified that you are owed a commission. If you run a YouTube channel or podcast, your affiliate will usually give you a code word to use in the sales cart or special section on their website to send your viewers/listeners to in order to purchase the product and have it registered as a referral sale. You will then be paid an agreed commission on the sales you have generated.

What Resources Do You Need?

You will only need the platform—website, blog, YouTube channel, or podcast—that you plan to use to host the affiliate links.

Advantages

Affiliate marketing is the truest form of passive income because once you have created the content, you leave the rest up to the consumers of your content. This method is extremely versatile and lends itself to any niche. The advantage for the merchant is that they are not paying for advertising unless they sell something. It is, therefore, relatively easy to convince merchants who are currently not using affiliate marketing to allow you to market their product in this way.

Disadvantages

The only disadvantages to affiliate marketing would be merchant-specific; for instance, with the Amazon affiliate program, you must sell three items within the first 180 days to remain in the program. Some merchants are quite specific about how much traffic your site must be getting to qualify for their affiliate program.

How Long Before I Make Money?

Generally, this will depend on the merchant as some will usually put a 60-day hold on paying out to facilitate any returns, and others will have a minimum threshold of commission that needs to be met to pay the marketer.

YouTube

What Is It?

YouTube is the largest video-sharing platform in the world. It has over 90 million users, and about 500 hours of video are uploaded to it every minute. Within this platform, you would create a channel to upload videos related to your content or niche. There are several ways to make passive income using YouTube.

How Does It Work?

The most common way to earn money from YouTube is through their advertisements. If you've ever watched a video on YouTube, you would have likely noticed that there are ads in the videos. The YouTube channel gets paid a fee for allowing those ads to appear in their videos. For any of the monetization features on YouTube, your channel must have at least 1000 subscribers and 4000 watch hours. You must also open a Google Adsense account. From there, you can become a YouTube Partner and take advantage of any of their monetization forms including ads, YouTube premium member commissions, channel memberships, and their merchandise shelf.

What Resources Do You Need?

You will need the resources required to record, edit, and upload high-quality videos to YouTube.

Advantages

After creating the original content, you don't really need to do anything else and you will generate passive income from many of the monetizations methods without doing any more work. If your YouTube channel works in tandem with your brand, then you are generating brand awareness and passive income in one go.

Disadvantages

YouTube is very strict about the type of content it will monetize. Anything that is seen as controversial could be demonetized. It takes some time to build up your subscribers and watch hours to YouTube's required level (Cooper, 2019).

How Long Before I Make Money?

This all depends on how long it takes you to get to YouTube's required number of subscribers and watch hours. Some channels manage it in weeks, and others take years. It will really depend on how much effort you put in to getting subscribers and encouraging them to watch your videos.

Dropshipping/Shopify

What Is It?

Dropshipping is a form of E-tail where the seller does not keep stock of the products themselves, but when they receive an order, they buy it online from a third-party and it is sent from that third-party to the customer. Shopify is an example of a dropship facilitation website.

How Does It Work?

The Shopify website provides you with a facility to open your online store. This store can be linked to your website, or it can stand alone on the Shopify website. Shopify has built-in services that help you to find product suppliers in your area or country. Once you have set up your E-store and arranged your suppliers, you can start advertising. As soon as you make your first sale, Shopify will facilitate the payment and make sure that both you and the supplier get paid.

What Resources Do You Need?

You would only need access to a computer and the internet to get started.

Advantages

By using dropshipping, you can test the market popularity of various products without actually having to stock them. Dropshipping saves the cost of buying products and warehousing them.

Disadvantages

Dealing with multiple suppliers can be tricky as their mistakes are your mistakes. When customers choose to purchase products from multiple different suppliers, the shipping costs can add up and you cannot pass that on to the customer if they have placed one order for all the items. You also make very low margins with dropshipping as there are many partners involved who need to get paid. Keeping track of inventory with dropshipping suppliers can be challenging.

How Long Before I Make Money?

This all depends on how long it takes to get your first customer, which in turn depends on how much you put into advertising and marketing (What is Dropshipping, n.d.).

Chapter 3: Why Affiliate Marketing Makes the Most Sense (and Dollars)

Now that we have looked at various methods we can use to generate passive income, we will focus on the method that is easiest to implement, the quickest to generate revenue, and has the biggest growth of all methods: affiliate marketing.

Eighty-one percent of brands in the United States use affiliate marketing to expand the reach of their products. This number is increasing by 10.1 percent each year, which means that by 2020, the affiliate marketing industry will be worth $6.8 billion.

As we explained in chapter 2, affiliate marketing is the process whereby an affiliate will promote a product in return for a set commission when a sale is generated from that promotion. The key to affiliate marketing is that the process leverages the strengths of various parties involved to spread the responsibility of sales generation. The three parties involved in affiliate marketing are:

- The merchant or seller, i.e., the party with the product for sale.
- The affiliate or promoter, i.e., the party with the platform where the product will be promoted.
- The customer, i.e., the party who will visit the platform of the affiliate and proceed to the merchant to purchase the product.

The merchant or seller can be a solo entrepreneur or a large company, and their product can be a physical item or a service. The affiliate or promotor can also take many forms, with the only requirement being that they have a platform to reach an audience to promote the product. Such platforms can include a website, blog, YouTube channel, or podcast. Social media influencers can also be affiliates. The consumer is the driving force behind affiliate marketing. Their purchases are the goal of both the merchant and the affiliate (Enfroy, 2019).

The access to a niche, targeted audience is the most significant difference between traditional advertising and affiliate marketing. When businesses use traditional marketing methods to promote their products, it is often a hit-or-miss affair. You may reach your audience, or you may not. With affiliate marketing, the merchant is choosing affiliates who have platforms that are already interacting with their target niche. The merchant is guaranteed to reach their target customers. Affiliate marketing works best if the affiliate is truly sold on the product they are promoting. Consumers can sense commitment and passion, and when an affiliate is excited about a product or service, it creates a sense of urgency to share in that excitement. In affiliate marketing, the merchant is also leveraging off relationships and reputations. If the affiliate has created the platform correctly, they should have an audience who values their input and that relationship becomes the selling point.

Therefore, as a future affiliate, your most important task in setting yourself up for future success in affiliate marketing is to create a platform that already provides value so that when you promote merchants, your audience will automatically see this as an additional value.

Up until this point, we have referenced a sale as the ultimate goal for the affiliate marketer to get paid, but this is not always the case. Depending on the merchant and the length of their sales cycle, they may be willing to pay you commission for helping them to reach other points in the sales funnel.

Some merchants will pay for leads. The nature of lead completion will differ. It could be that the merchant requires the customer to complete an application form or subscribe to a newsletter. If the customer clicks through your affiliate link to complete this action or uses a referral code issued to you, you will be paid an agreed amount for this lead.

Another method is pay per click or PPC. In this method of affiliate marketing, you will get paid if a customer clicks on an ad or link that takes them to the merchant's site. The most common example of PPC affiliate marketing is Google Adsense.

Affiliate marketing has several benefits, which include:

- The generation of passive income. Once you have established your platform and set up your content, there is very little else you need to do.

- No involvement in customer support. Dealing with the customer is the merchant's responsibility.
- Location freedom. You can run your affiliate marketing endeavors from anywhere in the world as long as you have an internet connection.
- Affiliate marketing is cost-effective for everyone. The merchant only pays you if you achieve the goal that has been set out in the agreement. The affiliate has very little capital outlay to get their affiliate marketing business going. The customer doesn't pay any more for the product through an affiliate link than they would if they went directly to the merchant themselves.

Different Platforms to Use for Affiliate Marketing

Blogs

Blogs are one of the most popular platforms for affiliate marketing. The reason for this is that the very nature of blogs means that there is a niche market reading the blog, and the blogger has a relationship with those readers. Depending on the topic, a good way to incorporate affiliate marketing is for the blogger to review products and then link to the merchant selling the product at the end of the review. Any successful blog has a well-defined niche, and that is the attraction for merchants who wish to use affiliate marketing on blogs.

Another benefit of using blogs as affiliate marketing partners is that blogs can rank organically on search engines, therefore increasing their reach.

Social Media Influencers

Social media influencers are people who have developed a position of power and influence in a specific industry and exert and display that influence predominantly on social media and YouTube. Such influencers are common in the makeup, fashion, food, and music industries. Through their influence they can impact the purchase decisions of their followers. When influencers conduct affiliate marketing for merchants, there is more than one benefit for both parties. The affiliate marketer, in this case, will often receive free products to try out so that they can recommend it. The merchant, besides the sale, has the image of their product elevated as these influencers are often well-respected.

Microsites

A microsite is, as the name suggests, a smaller version of a bigger website. It often takes a larger product segment and divides it into a single, targeted call-to-action. An example of a microsite is Spotify's "Year in Music," which pops up once a year around December to allow users to see which artists they listened to most that year and get other stats related to their geographical market.

Email Lists

Email lists are linked to another platform, such as a website or blog, where users have subscribed to the email list or newsletter of that site. The emails sent out are then structured around the affiliate marketing link, and recipients are encouraged to follow the links to the merchant's page.

Large Media Websites

Considering the high traffic that large media and news websites get, they are ideal for affiliate marketing, especially with intermittent ads between content (Enfroy, 2019).

Using Social Media to Drive Your Affiliate Marketing Business

Social media is one of the most powerful marketing tools in an affiliate marketer's toolbox. It is used to generate traffic to your site, engage with your content, and increase the likelihood that you will have a click-through to your merchant's site.

To effectively use social media, you must understand how it works and where to find your target audience. There are many different social media platforms including Twitter, Facebook, Instagram, and Pinterest. Each of those platforms serve a different niche, purpose, and encourage users to engage in different ways. The key to knowing which platform to use is understanding your own audience demographic. It may seem best to represent yourself on all social media platforms, but this is actually counterproductive. You will never be able to put the same amount of effort into five different platforms, and it is necessary to choose one or two and work them well.

The following are essential strategies to employ when using social media to promote your affiliate marketing business.

Consistency

Most social media platforms work on algorithms that push consistent posters. To begin with, you will only be seen in your own followers' news feeds. If you continue to post consistently, however, and occasionally boost posts, your reach will start to increase. To be consistent, you can plan a week's-worth of social media posts, create them, and save them as drafts. Some social media platforms give you the facility to schedule future posts, and there are programs that can be used to manage your social media posting on your behalf.

Images and Video

Social media users are proven to prefer posts with images and videos. Instagram and YouTube are the two biggest video promotion platforms in the world. Posts with images and videos are shown to have a far higher engagement than text-only posts. When using images, ensure that they represent a positive idea.

Content Must Be Engaging

You are not using social media to push your affiliate links. You are using social media to direct traffic to the platform that holds your affiliate links. When social media users see blatant adverts in posts, they often consider it to be spam. The key is to create posts that are providing users with information or entertainment that encourages them to find more of the same on your platform. As with any group of users, you need to develop a relationship with your social media followers, let them see that you are adding value to their lives, and engage them in content that will direct traffic. Trust and reputation are imperative in social media (Germain, n.d.).

Chapter 4: Getting Started with Affiliate Marketing

In the previous chapter, we provided you with a deeper dive into affiliate marketing. Affiliate marketing is one of the easiest ways to get started earning passive income, but just like any other method, you are going to need to put in the work before you receive the reward. Once you have decided what type of platform you are going to use—blog, website, microsite, YouTube channel, podcast, influencer—you need to find merchants to be an affiliate for. The most important consideration is that the merchant fits your product niche, but this is not to say that if you blog about gardening you can only engage in affiliate marketing for merchants who have gardening products. Your audience, as well as having a specific interest, also has a demographic—age, gender, occupation, income, and location—

which opens them up to other advertising that fits this demographic.

In looking for merchants to enter into affiliate marketing agreements, the greatest initial impact will come from affiliate networks.

What are Affiliate Networks

Affiliate networks are intermediaries that act as facilitators between affiliate marketers and merchants who wish to have their product or service promoted by affiliate marketers. They help each party to find the right fit for their platform or products. These networks are free to participate in, but they do generate their own revenue by taking either a share of the revenue earned by the affiliate marketer or charging a monthly subscription for the merchant to participate on their network.

An affiliate network will generally offer two ways for parties to generate revenue:

- Sharing revenue: the affiliate partner earns a share of the revenue generated by the sale that the merchant makes as a result of the affiliate partner's promotion.
- Fee for action: this is where the affiliate partner gets a set fee when a customer completes a specific action, e.g., PPC (Tipalti, n.d.).

Examples of Popular Affiliate Networks

Clickfunnels™ is a software program for online businesses to help increase their sales and market their products. Clickfunnels also has an affiliate network where you can promote the Clickfunnels products and generate income when one of the visitors to your platform use the services of Clickfunnels. The company offers a 40 % commission on the sales of Clickfunnels products or services, which is paid to the affiliate after a 45-day cooling-off period—to cover any refunds or returns. To become a Clickfunnels affiliate, you need to be a paying member of Clickfunnels (BigFoot Digital, n.d.).

Clickbank is the original affiliate network. It was established in 1998 and has 200 million customers across 190 countries. Clickbank is one of the easiest methods of affiliate marketing, which is why it is a good place for beginners to start. Its sign-up process is quick and easy, and you can use Clickbank as an affiliate marketer or a merchant. Clickbank has a large selection of products that you can be an affiliate for, and it pays high commissions. As with anything, though, there are some challenges with the network, including notoriously slow customer service. Another downside is that Clickbank charges you if your account is dormant and you make no sales within a specific period. If you want to start with Clickbank, be sure that you are representing products and brands with a good reputation and that you believe in. Keep in mind that by being an affiliate, you are linking your name to that product or service, and if things go wrong, your reputation could be impacted as well. Try the product and check online reviews. You should also do some research on the merchant in question to ensure that you are satisfied that they are a reputable brand (Nyathi, 2019).

JVZoo is another affiliate marketing network that leverages off the fact that its services are instantaneous. A benefit of JVZoo is that the tracking cookies last longer than 24-hours after your user has clicked the link. With JVZoo, your referral is automatically linked to any purchase that customer makes in the future too. So you don't just commission on one sale, you will receive a commission on anything they buy from that merchant in the future as well. JVZoo also pays instantly. As soon as the customer completes a purchase through your referral link, you will receive your commission. Should the customer request a refund at any time, you will be required to refund the commission paid to you. JVZoo only uses PayPal to pay affiliate marketers, so if you do not have access to PayPal you won't be able to use JVZoo. You need to apply to each JVZoo vendor separately, which could be time-consuming, depending on how many products you plan to be an affiliate for (Hofmann, n.d.).

How to Get Traffic to Your Platform

There are various methods of driving traffic to your platform, some of which we have already touched on:

- Paid advertising - this can include Google ads and ads on social media.
- Social media - we discussed this method in detail in Chapter 3.
- If you have a blog, try varying the length of your content to see what attracts more traffic.
- Write compelling headlines for your content.
- Optimize search engine optimization (SEO) techniques.
- Use popular keywords.
- Guest blogging - network with other blogs in your niche and write posts for them that will drive their readers to your site as well.
- Try LinkedIn - this platform is now much more than a job-hunting website (Shewan, 2019).
- YouTube channel - even if you are not monetizing through YouTube yet, you can use the platform to direct traffic to your site.
- If you have used the Kindle Direct Publishing service to publish a book,

this is also an excellent way to drive traffic to your site.

How to Build a Landing Page that Converts

What is a Landing Page?

A landing page is a static page that is a part of your website or blog. It is usually the main entry-point for visitors to your platform, and it should provide them with a call-to-action to convert them to regular visitors to your page or to perform a specific action, such as reading a very specific piece of content or signing up to a newsletter. Getting the visitor to engage with your call-to-action is called 'conversion.' Conversion rates differ between niches, but the average conversion rate is about 3 %. Ideally, you want to be aiming for higher than average, which is around 11 %.

How to Encourage Conversion

There are various ways to encourage conversion, including the following:

- Use a single call-to-action. Make your intention for the visitor very clear, and only ask them to do one thing. You could be asking them to subscribe to a newsletter or click through to your latest content post. The instruction must be clear and easy to follow.
- The call-to-action must stand out on the landing page. Use contrasting colors and language that encourages action.
- Ensure that your call-to-action is in the line of sight as soon as a visitor arrives on your landing page. The should not have to scroll to find it.
- You will need to offer something in exchange for your visitor's conversion, and it needs to be valuable. A free document, book, course, or template can provide the value needed to secure their conversion.
- Include your unique value proposition. This is a statement that explains to your visitor how you plan

to solve their problem or add value to their lives.

- Let people know how to get into contact with you. Social media information usually works well here.
- Include some great reviews or testimonials of your site.
- Your grammar and spelling must be absolutely flawless on your landing page. Any errors will cause your visitor to wonder about the validity of your page.
- Don't overload the page. Too much information on your landing page is going to be confusing and drag your visitor's attention away from your call-to-action (Swain, 2018).

Low-Ticket vs. High-Ticket

An important consideration in setting up your affiliate marketing business is deciding whether you will be offering low-ticket or high-ticket products i.e., affordable or high-end.

Predominantly, this is going to depend on your niche. If you are marketing to parents of toddlers, they are likely already cash-strapped, so your best bet is marketing low-ticket items. If you are marketing to foodies who enjoy top-class food and restaurants, you can look at higher ticketed items. It is best to have a range and test out different prices to see what your audience is interested in. Even if your niche lends itself to higher ticketed items, it is always best to offer a lower cost alternative as well. Generally, people will only buy high-ticket items from businesses they know, so if you offer a lower cost version, you will be able to secure the customer for your merchant. Once that customer has used and enjoyed the product, they will likely come back for a higher ticketed item. You will usually sell more low-ticket items, so there is a possibility that you could generate more revenue by marketing low-ticket items than high-ticket items. High-ticket items, on the other hand, will give you a higher revenue in one go. The decision is always going to be based on your audience and their needs, so be sure to be intuitive about that when making the decision on the price range of products you will offer (Bullock, 2017).

Chapter 5: Strategizing for Your Selected Affiliate Business

In Chapter 4, we briefly discussed Clickfunnels and their affiliate network. In this chapter, we will delve deeper into this phenomenal software and discuss not only how it can help you make money from an affiliate perspective but also how it can be used to help you strategize for your online business as a whole.

Clickfunnels is a software package. It is not to be mistaken with a sales funnel, which is the sales jargon term for the process we place prospects in our business with the intention that they will be converted into new customers on the other end of that funnel. For non-digital businesses, a sales funnel will include events like meetings, presentations, and methods of closing the customer face-to-face. For online businesses, as we will only ever interact with our customers online, a sales funnel is the digital process we take our new visitors through to convert them into buying customers. Clickfunnels helps you to build sales funnels.

The biggest difference between any business' standard website and the development of a website with Clickfunnels is that if you go to a standard business website, you will find information on their products, who they are as a business, and where they operate. You will likely browse that website for a few minutes and then click out of it because there is no clear path for you to follow to any call-to-action. A website developed with Clickfunnels is built to guide you from the entry point through to the point of sale.

Clickfunnels does not build a website for you; it builds a sales funnel. If you go to the landing page of a site developed using Clickfunnels, you will not find the standard menus you would find on other websites such as 'about,' 'products,' 'services,' and "contact us." This is because a menu like this gives you too many options and with online businesses, options are the equivalent of distractions, and distractions lose sales.

When you access the landing page of a site built by Clickfunnels, you will find one available action—the call-to-action we discussed previously. Once you click on that call-to-action, the next step in the sales funnel will be a sales page where the customer can view information about the product that you are selling and enter their payment information. Clickfunnels helps you to add what is called an 'upsell' to the payment cart. An upsell is when your customer is already in buying mode, and you add something else to the package that increases the value to the customer and increases your revenue. An example could be a book that you are selling, and when your customer goes to purchase the book they receive an upsell request to also purchase your online course at a discounted rate. After your customer has committed to purchasing and entered their information, they will be taken to a full sales page that may include your high-ticket items. Clickfunnels saves the customer's purchase information (for that transaction only, not permanently) and if they click on any of your high-ticket items, it will automatically bill them. The reason for this is that, from a psychological perspective, if a customer has to enter their payment information a second time, they are far more likely to abandon the sale. The button that your customers click to buy high-ticket items has a disclaimer written on it that warns if they click that button they will be automatically billed.

Should the customer not wish to purchase the high-ticket item at that time, Clickfunnels inserts an option for them to decline the transaction, which takes them to a lower-cost alternative. The last step after all the sales pages is a thank you page that will either provide your customer with a free item you may have offered, or it provides links to follow you on social media. The idea behind Clickfunnels is to maximize your sales from your traffic but also to maximize the value you provide your customers (Buildapreneur, 2018).

Clickfunnels is the key to maximizing your marketing efforts. Not only is it a far easier way to build a sales site that is geared toward converting customers, once you are sold on it as a product and you can see its value in real terms, you can join their affiliate program and help others to improve their businesses while earning an affiliate commission.

Clickfunnels Affiliate Program

One you have used Clickfunnels in your online business, you are going to be sold on its value. When you are passionate about a product, it is much easier to sell.

Before we get into the specifics behind the Clickfunnels affiliate program, let us first cover a few terms that are used within the program which are important to understand:

- **Trial** - Clickfunnels offers a free 14-day trial. If you get someone to sign-up to a trial, Clickfunnels is not yet making any money and, therefore, neither do you. After the 14 days are up, however, they will need to either subscribe to Clickfunnels or forfeit the program. When they subscribe, you will earn money.
- **Monthly Recurring Revenue (MRR)** - Because Clickfunnels is a software program, the user is charged for the services they use on a monthly basis, which can be anywhere between $97 and $297 and the MRR comes in when you earn 40 % of that each month as an affiliate.

- **Churn** - This is not only an online business term but also a standard sales term. It means how many people naturally drop off from the program every month. This could happen for many reasons and may not have anything to do with something you or Clickfunnels has done. It is a very normal part of the sales process.
- **Painkiller or Vitamin** - You want to be marketing products that are painkillers and not vitamins. Vitamins are nice to have, but they are not necessary, whereas painkillers are necessary if you want to live a pain-free life. In other words, you want to be marketing a product that gives your customers a solution to their problem. Clickfunnels is a painkiller.

Once you are a paying member of Clickfunnels, you automatically qualify to be an affiliate. The following will guide to accessing your Clickfunnels affiliate account.

Inside the software, go to your profile picture, hold your mouse over it and you will see a tab labeled 'affiliate.' You will be taken to a page that will show you your earnings, and underneath it is all of the options of the various Clickfunnels products you can market.

Underneath the options, there is a button that reads, "Get My Affiliate Links." This takes you to the links that you will use to guide customers to the Clickfunnels website via your link and log their purchase as a sale for your affiliate account.

Once you have decided which of the Clickfunnels products you are going to market, you click on the "affiliate links" button, and it will take you to a page where you can copy your affiliate link. This link is embedded into your site.

Clickfunnels provides you with a host of marketing material to use in your campaign such as banner ads, instagram posts, and email ads.

Clickfunnels is the ultimate passive income generator because once you have signed someone up, you will earn that monthly recurring commission without doing anything else. Clickfunnels also has additional rewards for their affiliates besides their monthly commissions. Their current additional reward is that any affiliate who has more than 100 recurring subscribers on their account receives $500 per month toward their dream car. If you reach 200 recurring subscribers, you receive $1000 per month toward your dream car.

Clickfunnels also provides different products geared toward different audiences, for instance, if you happen to have a predominantly female audience, Clickfunnels has a product specifically designed for female E-preneurs. It is important to market Clickfunnels as a software program that solves the problems of online entrepreneurs. If you attempt to market Clickfunnels as a way to *start* a business, you are likely to have a far higher churn rate because that is a misrepresentation of what the product does. A good way to do this is by promoting Clickfunnels free 14-day trial. By doing this, you are promoting the software and nothing else.

Once you start signing customers up, the Clickfunnels affiliate page provides you with a wide range of statistics and numbers that you can use to manage your affiliate program.

The monthly recurring income generated from Clickfunnels is the key to your financial freedom. You don't just want one-of payments. Passive income needs to generate itself consistently, and that is exactly what Clickfunnels does (Crestani, 2019).

Conclusion

As the world changes, the economy changes with it. We can no longer rely solely on one company to provide us with the money we need to fund our lives and support our families. We have no choice but to start thinking outside the box. The world of passive income generation can be intimidating when you first look at it. How can it even be possible to earn money without actively working something every day?

Models of passive income have existed for many decades. Rental income and commission earned by financial consultants can both be considered forms of passive income. What we have done in this book is to convert that idea into online possibilities.

As with starting any business, you will need an entrepreneurial mindset, and let's be honest, not everyone is cut out to be an entrepreneur. Some people are far happier working for a boss at their 9 to 5 jobs, and there's really nothing wrong with if it makes you happy. It is risky to rely 100 percent on a

9 to 5 job with no back-up income. Circumstances can change in a second, and in the current economy, we have seen large businesses shut down overnight. If you think that you would be better off as a 9 to 5 worker, ask yourself, what would you do if you drove to work tomorrow morning and your employer had closed its doors? Everyone should have a back-up income whether you plan on being a permanent online entrepreneur or not.

We covered five of the most popular ways to generate passive income online. The method you choose is going to be based on your interests and skills as well as the audience you are trying to reach. Really, the smartest method is to try to include as many of these methods as possible, but we all have to start somewhere and affiliate marketing is the best place to start.

Traffic is key for online businesses. You want to draw traffic to your site, and you want to convert that traffic. We discussed the ways that social media can be used to drive traffic to your website. Remember, you cannot expect to be highly successful on every social media platform that exists. You must pick one or two that fits your audience and work those platforms hard. Once you've managed to generate traffic, you want to convert them through your landing page. We've provided you with some great tips on how to build a successful conversion landing page. Think about the last time you purchased something online. Now go to that business' landing page and analyze it. Ask yourself what made you want to interact with that page and how they drew you into the purchase. Now apply those elements to your own landing page.

We discussed the basics behind affiliate marketing—how to get started, what the different platforms are that can be used, and what affiliate networks are. We then took a deep dive into the quintessential passive income generation program—Clickfunnels. We discovered how we can use Clickfunnels to generate recurring monthly income all while adding value to our customers. The latter is a point you really want to focus on in your passive income generation journey. You don't want to just be selling 'stuff' for the sake of it. That will only serve to create a reputation for you that you are someone who only cares about making money, and you don't really care whether you are adding value or selling a reputable product. That may earn you a few sales, but in the long-term, it is going to damage your potential. Customers want to know that the person selling to them really cares about them and wants to sell them a product that is useful, valuable, and will solve their problems. That is also where relationship-building comes in. You cannot expect to open a website and start selling. You need to build relationships first.

In *How to Make Money on the Internet,* we have provided you with a way to circumvent the traditional, active income model. We have given you the keys to your financial, time, and location freedom. All you need to do now is take those keys and open the door.

References

23 tips for building a landing page that converts in 2018 - Agile CRM Blog. (2018, August 10). Retrieved December 10, 2019, from Agile CRM Blog website: https://www.agilecrm.com/blog/building-a-landing-page-that-converts/

25 Ways to Increase Traffic to Your Website. (2014). Retrieved December 10, 2019, from Wordstream.com website: https://www.wordstream.com/blog/ws/2014/08/14/increase-traffic-to-my-website

Anderson, V. (2018, June 20). An Inside Look at the Mindset of a Successful Entrepreneur. Retrieved December 10, 2019, from Oberlo website: https://www.oberlo.com/blog/mindset-successful-entrepreneur

Ayodeji Awosika. (2019, March 21). Kindle Direct Publishing: How to Make Real Money on Amazon. Retrieved December 10, 2019, from Smart Blogger website: https://smartblogger.com/kindle-publishing/#common_questions

E-preneur: The Growth of Online Entrepreneurship Infographic. (2015). Retrieved December 10, 2019, from Lucrazon.com website: http://www.lucrazon.com/growth-of-online-entrepreneurship

Gennifer Carragher. (2018, December 12). Amazon FBA in 2019: How It Works (Benefits + Disadvantages). Retrieved December 10, 2019, from The BigCommerce Blog website: https://www.bigcommerce.com/blog/amazon-fba/#14-tactics-to-successfully-sell-on-amazon-fba

How Does Clickfunnels Affiliate Program Work? [YouTube Video]. (2019). Retrieved from https://www.youtube.com/watch?v=NBCoZb6g0ok

How to Make Money on YouTube: 6 Effective Strategies. (2019, August 8). Retrieved December 10, 2019, from Hootsuite Social Media Management website: https://blog.hootsuite.com/how-to-make-money-on-youtube/

How To Make Money With Clickfunnels: Becoming A Clickfunnels Affiliate. (2016). Retrieved December 10, 2019, from SEO Company in Barnsley | Social Media Marketing Agency in Yorkshire website: https://www.bigfootdigital.co.uk/clickfunnels-affiliate-program

https://www.facebook.com/adamenfroydotcom. (2018, July 27). Affiliate Marketing in 2019: What It Is + How Beginners Can Start. Retrieved December 10, 2019, from The BigCommerce Blog website: https://www.bigcommerce.com/blog/affiliate-marketing/#how-does-affiliate-marketing-work

https://www.facebook.com/meetana. (2012, September 4). Ana Hoffman. Retrieved December 10, 2019, from TrafficGenerationCafe.com website: https://trafficgenerationcafe.com/jvzoo-affiliate-marketing/

Lilach Bullock. (2017, May 19). High ticket vs low ticket – which is more valuable to your business? Retrieved from LilachBullock website: https://www.lilachbullock.com/high-ticket-sales-low-ticket/

Pj Germain. (2019, June 18). How to Use Social Media to Drive Your Affiliate Marketing. Retrieved December 10, 2019, from Pure Residuals website: https://pureresiduals.com/how-to-use-social-media-to-drive-your-affiliate-marketing/

Qhubekani Nyathi. (2019, July 24). ClickBank: The Brutally Honest, Must-Read Guide for 2020. Retrieved December 10, 2019, from Smart Blogger website: https://smartblogger.com/clickbank/

What EXACTLY Is ClickFunnels - An Inside Look [YouTube Video]. (2018). Retrieved from https://www.youtube.com/watch?v=9T92osOWYkE

What is an affiliate network? (2015). Retrieved December 10, 2019, from Tipalti website: https://tipalti.com/customers/affiliate-networks-tipalti/what-is-an-affiliate-network/

What Is Dropshipping | How Does Drop Shipping Work? (2016). Retrieved December 10, 2019, from Shopify website:

https://www.shopify.co.za/guides/dropship
ping/understanding-dropshipping